ACID RAIN

John Baines

Conserving Our World

Acid Rain
Conserving Rainforests
Waste and Recycling
Conserving the Atmosphere
Protecting Wildlife
The Spread of Deserts

Cover: Acid rain is likely to have contributed to the
death of these trees in northern USA.

Series editor: Sue Hadden
Series designer: Ross George

First published in 1989 by
Wayland (Publishers) Ltd
61 Western Road, Hove
East Sussex BN3 1JD, England

British Library Cataloguing in Publication Data
Baines, John D. (John David), 1943 –
  Acid rain.
  1. Environment. Pollution by acid rain
  – For children.
  I. Title II Series
  363.7'386

ISBN 1–85210–694–8

Typeset by Lizzie George, Wayland
Printed and bound in Italy by Sagdos S.p.A., Milan.

Contents

Introduction

An encounter with a lifeless lake

Our journey through the Swedish forest was almost over. The Ecobus, which had carried our party of European teachers along the bumpy forest road, came to a halt. We got out and walked through the fir trees to a clearing. Suddenly we were faced by a most beautiful lake. The water was so clear and still that the trees and blue sky were reflected in it perfectly. About 12 m below the surface, the bottom of the lake was clearly visible – in fact it was more like looking through air than water.

I sat quietly by the lake and marvelled at the beauty of nature. Then, slowly, a feeling of unease came over me. It was too quiet and too calm. Why were there no birds swimming on the lake? Where were all the water plants that are normally found growing in lakes like this? Surely there must be some small fish in the lake, or some troublesome midges hovering above the surface? But there was nothing to see at all. Suddenly I realized the truth. Our Swedish host had brought us to an acidified lake that had no life in it because of acid rain. Now the lake was no longer beautiful. It was an ugly example of what people can do to the environment.

This Canadian scene may look very beautiful but the lake contains little life. The clear water suggests that the lake may be suffering from the effects of acid rain.

In Sweden there are hundreds of acidified lakes like this. They have been harmed mostly by acid rain caused by other countries, which has been carried over Sweden by the wind. Acid rain is caused by burning fossil fuels like coal and oil and allowing them to pollute the atmosphere. This form of pollution is so strong that many trees and lakes are dying, buildings are decaying and, in some cases, people's health is being damaged.

Acid rain is one of many pressures on our environment caused by the modern way of life enjoyed by people in the more industrialized countries. Modern technology has made many people richer, more healthy and more comfortable than ever before. However, all these benefits depend on our environment, which provides us with everything we need – the air we

Rainwater is not always as pure as it looks. When acid raindrops fall on trees or into lakes, they can cause a build-up of acidity, which leads to serious problems.

breathe, the water we drink and the food we eat, the house in which we live and the school in which we learn. If we continue to damage the environment, then it will not be able to support us so well.

In the following chapters, we will learn more about acid rain and how it can damage the environment. We will also look at the ways in which this problem is being tackled, and ask what we all can do to make sure that the world remains a pleasant place in which to live. After all, it is the only one we have.

How the environment becomes acid

Few people in Europe or North America have not heard of 'acid rain'. The words are used frequently in the press and on television. Acid rain is widely recognized as a cause of serious environmental problems, especially in forests and lakes. The term is used because it is a very dramatic and simple way of describing a very complicated problem. Environmental groups generally talk of 'acid precipitation', which includes snow, mist and hail, as well as rain.

How acid is rainwater?

When water evaporates from the sea, lakes or the land, the moisture is neither acid nor alkaline. It is neutral. However, the moisture absorbs gases like carbon dioxide found in the atmosphere, and becomes a weak acid. Natural rainfall has a pH of between 5 and 6 (neutral is pH7). It can dissolve rocks and create spectacular limestone caves, gorges and pinnacles, in a process that takes thousands of years.

Rain can dissolve limestone into strange shapes, such as these Australian pinnacles.

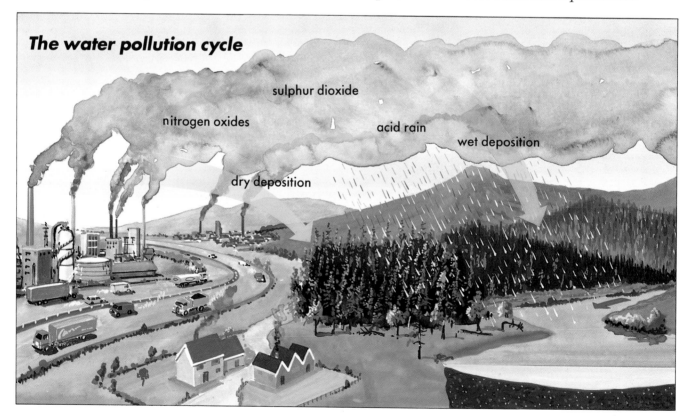

The water pollution cycle

sulphur dioxide

nitrogen oxides

acid rain

wet deposition

dry deposition

Acids and alkalis are opposites

Normally we think of acids in their strong forms when they can be very dangerous. However, they can be neutralized until they are no more acid than lemon juice, vinegar or a drink of cola.

Alkalis are the opposite of acids, although in their concentrated form, they too can cause damage. Old wooden furniture is often placed in a bath of caustic soda to remove layers of paint and reveal the natural wood beneath. Less powerful alkalis are used in the home regularly including washing soda and bicarbonate of soda.

If you add an acid to an alkali, the concentration of both is reduced. By carefully controlling the amounts added, it is possible for a mixture to become neither acid nor alkaline, but neutral.

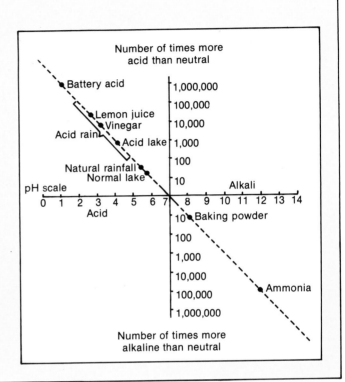

Measuring acidity

There is a scale for describing the strength of an acid or alkaline solution. It is called the pH scale. The scale extends from zero (very acid) to fourteen (alkaline). The neutral point is seven. Remember, therefore, when pH values are given in this book, that pH 4.5 is more acidic than pH 5.

The pH scale is a logarithmic one. If there are 3 samples, **A** with a pH of 6.5, **B** 5.5 and **C** 4.5, then **B** is ten times more acid than **A, C** is 100 times more acid than **A** and 10 times more acid than **B**. An increase in acidity by one unit really means a tenfold increase in acidity.

There are various ways of measuring acidity. A cheap way is to use litmus papers. These are narrow strips of coloured paper. When dipped into a solution, the paper turns either red, for acids, or blue, for alkalis. When using Universal Indicator papers (shown below), you can determine the pH of the sample.

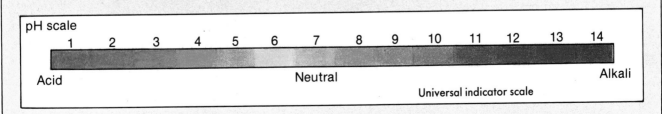

Natural events can increase the acidity of rainfall. When volcanoes erupt explosively, they release many gases into the atmosphere. Some of these are absorbed by the moisture in the atmosphere and fall as acid rain, but their impact is usually only short-lived.

Air pollution

Most air pollution is caused as a result of burning fossil fuels like coal and oil. These fuels have been formed over thousands of years from dead

__Above__ The spectacular sight of Mount Augustine erupting in Alaska. When volcanoes erupt, they pour many gases into the air, including sulphur dioxide. However, natural events like these only cause about 10% of air pollution – the rest is caused by human activities.

__Right__ Power stations, like this one in Maryland, USA, burn fossil fuel to produce energy. Many gases are released into the atmosphere, some of which cause acid rain.

Making 'acid rain'

Put some distilled water in the jar and measure its pH value with Universal Indicator paper. Light four matches carefully and put them into the jar of water, keeping the lid slightly open. Let the matches extinguish and then remove them from the jar, closing the lid. Shake the jar so that the water thoroughly absorbs the fumes from the matches. The paper should now have turned reddish-orange because the water has become acidified.

Add some crushed chalk to the solution and shake again. The paper should turn bluish-green because the alkaline chalk will overcome the acid solution.

This experiment simulates acid rain because the burning matches produce sulphur and phosphorous, which are also emitted from chimney smoke. When they mix with rainwater it becomes acid rain.

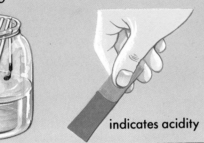

indicates acidity

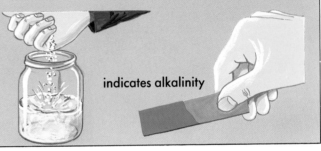

indicates alkalinity

plants and animals. Deposits built up and were eventually covered by other rocks and compressed. They remained almost untouched until the middle of the eighteenth century. Since then they have been used in ever-increasing amounts to drive machines, heat buildings and smelt metals like iron.

When the fuel is burnt, not only is the energy released, but many other chemicals as well, including sulphur and nitrogen that the organic material contained. These substances are two of the most important ingredients of acid rain. Sulphur and nitrogen are unwanted by-products from the burning of fuels, and so generally they are discharged directly into the atmosphere where they disperse safely, or so it was thought. We now know this is not the case. They convert rapidly into sulphur dioxide and nitrogen oxides which most people agree damage the environment.

The amounts that are discharged into the atmosphere are astonishing: around 24 million tonnes of sulphur dioxide a year in North America and 44 million tonnes in Europe. That is enough to fill about 150 supertankers! Most of the sulphur comes from factories and power stations generating electricity.

The quantity of nitrogen oxides produced is smaller, but still amounts to 22 million tonnes in North America and 15 million tonnes in western Europe. Emissions from vehicle engines form most of the nitrogen oxides. As traffic increases by as much as 20 per cent a year in Europe, the problem is likely to become worse unless immediate action is taken.

What happens to air pollution?

Some of the pollution falls to the ground very quickly, before it is absorbed by moisture. It settles on trees, buildings and lakes, usually in the area where it was produced. This is called 'dry deposition'. These deposits build up and later combine with rainwater to become acids.

The rest of the pollution can remain in the air for up to a week and is carried long distances by the wind. During this time, the chemicals react with the moisture in the atmosphere and become dilute sulphuric and nitric acids. They are ready to become acid rain. They also react with other chemicals in the atmosphere to form secondary pollutants. Ozone is one of the most dangerous of these, as it damages vegetation.

When acid precipitation falls as snow, the problems for the environment are delayed, but can be much worse eventually. During the winter, the snow collects on the ground, holding on to its acids. In spring, when the snow melts,

During the spring thaw, the acidity of rivers is much higher. This photograph shows snow melt in British Columbia, Canada.

there is a sudden surge of water which flows across the land into streams and lakes. Sometimes six months' store of acids is released in a few weeks. These 'acid surges', as they are called, are particularly harmful to plants and animals.

Farming and forestry

Air pollution is not the only cause of the environment becoming more acidic. As plants grow, they take up and use nutrients from the soil. This increases the acidity of the soil. When the plants die, they rot back into the soil, returning the nutrients and reducing the acidity. Nature has created its own cycle for maintaining

When trees are felled for timber, their nutrients are not returned to the soil. This makes the soil more acid and less able to support future generations of trees. The photograph shows piles of timber in Finland, where forestry is an important industry.

stable pH levels. In farming, the plants are removed for food and in forestry the trees are removed for timber. So the nutrients are not returned to the soil to reduce the acidity. To maintain the fertility of the soil, artificial fertilizers are used, especially nitrates. However, these can further increase the acidity of the soil, therefore making the problem even worse.

Air pollution and the wind

As long ago as 1661, scientists in Britain found that industrial pollution could affect the health of people and plants in the surrounding area. As industry grew in the eighteenth and nineteenth centuries, damage to people's health and to the environment increased. However, no one thought that the pollution was carried very far. Then in 1881, a Norwegian scientist found what he called 'dirty fall-out' on the west coast of Norway where there was no polluting industry. He suspected that it came from Britain. Today scientists have proved beyond doubt that pollution is carried very long distances in the air. If any further proof was needed, then it was provided by the accident at the Soviet nuclear power station, Chernobyl, which led to radioactive rain falling over areas of eastern and western Europe. The effects of this radioactive rain on the environment may last for decades.

Scandinavian countries had recognized that acid rain was one of the chief causes of their lakes becoming acidified. Much research has been undertaken to show the significant links between sulphur dioxide depositions and environmental damage. Following this evidence,

Factories like this one in Cumbria, Britain, release smoke into the air, where it is carried long distances by the wind.

most countries have agreed to reduce their emissions. Some countries, however, are doing so grudgingly and say that more conclusive evidence is needed to prove that sulphur dioxide causes extensive damage to the environment.

How far can pollution be carried?

If you look at smoke coming from a chimney, there are very few days in the year when it goes straight up. Most often, the smoke bends away from the chimney because the air around the chimney is moving. Even when there appears to be only a slight wind on the ground, higher up it can be much stronger.

The pollution from the chimneys is carried by the wind. Some of it may stay in the air for a week or more before it is deposited on the ground. In that time it can have travelled many kilometres. Even a gentle wind of 16 kilometres per hour could carry the pollution over 1,600 kilometres in

Acid rain in North America

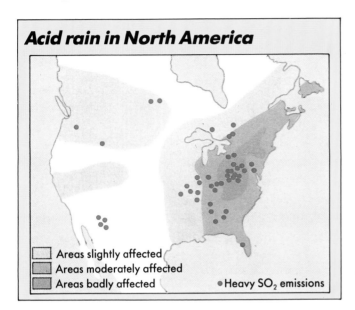

Areas slightly affected
Areas moderately affected
Areas badly affected
● Heavy SO₂ emissions

The above map shows the extent of acid rain in North America and gives areas of high sulphur dioxide emissions.

Right *The three diagrams show how sulphur dioxide pollution produced in Europe affects Scandinavian countries.* **Diagram 1** *shows levels of sulphur dioxide pollution produced in western Europe.* **Diagram 2** *shows how winds carry pollution from Europe to Scandinavia.* **Diagram 3** *shows areas affected by acid rain.*

five days. The longer the pollution stays in the atmosphere, the more its chemical composition changes. It becomes a complicated cocktail of pollutants that damage the environment.

In the major industrial areas of the northern hemisphere, the prevailing wind (the one that blows most often) is from the west. This means that places downwind of these industrial areas receive the worst pollution. Every year about 3 million tonnes of acid pollution is blown into Canada from the USA. Of all the sulphur dioxide deposited in eastern Canada, 50 per cent comes from the industrial areas of northeast USA. In Europe, the acid pollution is blown into Scandinavia from the surrounding countries, especially Britain and eastern Europe.

How acid rain affects Scandinavia

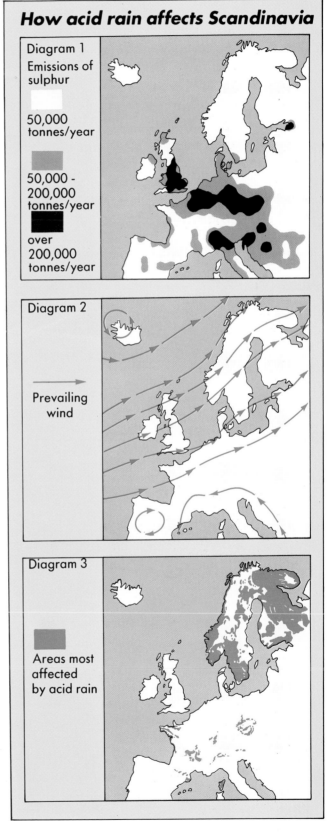

Diagram 1
Emissions of sulphur

50,000 tonnes/year

50,000 - 200,000 tonnes/year

over 200,000 tonnes/year

Diagram 2

Prevailing wind

Diagram 3

Areas most affected by acid rain

Why is it that in the county of Telemark in southern Norway, some of the lakes are badly affected by acid rain, and some, only a few kilometres away, are not? Why are the forests close to some industrial areas not as badly damaged by acid rain as those thousands of miles away? The answer lies in the soil.

Soils are formed when rock is broken up by the weather and erosion, and mixed with organic matter from plants and animals. Without soil, most plants cannot grow. The rocks from which the soil is made may be acid, neutral or alkaline.

Chalk and limestone are rocks that are made from tiny shells that are rich in calcium. Calcium is alkaline and the soils that develop on these rocks are usually alkaline as well. When acid rain falls on alkaline soil, the acid is made weaker, or neutralized, and there are few environmental problems.

Granite is a very hard acidic rock that breaks up very slowly. The soils are usually very thin, but they are able to reduce the acidity of normal rain to a level that plants and animals can tolerate. A balance is maintained. Acid rain overloads this natural system and gradually the environment becomes too acid for the plants and animals to remain healthy. A new balance is eventually reached, but at a level that cannot support such a rich variety of plants and animals.

Chalk soils support a wide variety of plants. Chalk also counteracts the effects of acid rain.

Granite soils can be badly affected by acid rain, so that eventually fewer plants and animals can survive on them.

The effect of soils on acid rain

Collect a number of soil samples in bin liners from different areas in the locality. Make a funnel from an old plastic bottle by cutting off its bottom. Place a filter paper in the upturned bottle and fill it with soil. Make a solution of water and vinegar with pH value 4.0. Pour it over the soil sample slowly and collect the water in a beaker as it drips through. Measure its pH value and record it. Repeat the experiment with different soil samples to see how much each one can buffer the acidity of the solution.

Testing soil samples

Animals and plants in areas affected by acid rain have other problems too. Soils naturally contain small amounts of poisonous minerals like aluminium, cadmium and mercury. Normally they do not cause serious problems, but as the acidity of the soil increases, chemical reactions allow the minerals to be absorbed by plants. The plants are then damaged and any animals eating them will absorb the poisons, which remain in their body. The harmful minerals are also leached out of the soil into streams and lakes, where they can kill fish and other living creatures. The problems become greater when pollution dumps yet more minerals into the soil. In parts of Poland, vegetable crops have been found to contain ten times more lead than is considered safe.

15

Acidity in lakes

One of the most popular hobbies in North America and Europe is fishing in lakes and streams. It is enjoyed by millions of people and there is hardly a lake, stream or river that is not used by anglers. Fishing is also big business. Not only are fishing rights sold to angling clubs, but many people are employed in commercial fishing, especially for salmon and trout. Fish farming has become an important economic activity in many remote areas, offering much-needed employment to local people. Their livelihood is threatened by acid rain.

About 90 per cent of the water in lakes and streams has previously passed through the ground. As the ability of the soil to weaken the acids has fallen, and the acidity of the rainfall has

This Swedish lake has a pH of 5.2, which is harmful to some kinds of fish and other freshwater creatures.

Lake damage

'Like many Norwegians, we have a summer house in the hills by a lake. We used to eat a lot of fish that we caught in the streams and lakes. Recently, we have been advised not to eat them, as they contain poisonous metals that have been washed out of the soil and into the water'.

Ulf Pederson

Contaminated water supplies

'My family lives in the Swedish countryside and we always used to get our water from a shallow well near the house. My father used to keep a fish in the well to eat any worms that fell into it. We first noticed something was wrong when the fish we put in kept dying. When we measured the pH level, we found that it was 4.9. We also found that the pipes in the house were rotting and we had to replace them all. Some people came to drill a deeper well, but now this has got too acid also and we have had to install a filter. Fortunately we were able to get a grant from the government to help pay for it.'

Astrid Fjortoft

A healthy lake teems with wildlife, both above and below the surface. Here a dragonfly rests on a water lily.

Acidification of lakes - some facts:

- In the southern area of Norway, it is estimated that 90 per cent of all trout will have been lost by 1990.

- In the spring thaw of 1984, very acid water with pH 3.8 was recorded in the Vikadel River in Norway.

- Up to 80 per cent of the 700,000 lakes in eastern Canada are acid or becoming so.

- Fish have disappeared from more than 200 lakes in the Adirondack Mountains of New York State, USA.

increased, the acidity of the water in the lakes and streams has also increased. Lakes also receive rainfall direct from the sky. There is no chance for the acidity of this water to be reduced by the soil. The situation has become steadily worse in the most sensitive areas of North America and Europe since 1950, although there is evidence that conditions are stabilizing.

A healthy lake has a pH around 6.5 and is able to support a variety of plants, insects and fish. In addition, there are a number of animals and birds that feed on the plentiful food in a healthy lake.

The Osprey

The osprey is a large bird of prey which flies low over the surface of a lake and picks fish out of the water with its claws. It is becoming rare in Europe and there is now great concern for its future, as 60 per cent of all the breeding pairs in Europe are found in Sweden. If the fish disappear from the Swedish lakes because of acid rain, the osprey too will disappear.

As the pH of the lake falls (the level of acidity rises) the fish find it more difficult to reproduce successfully. Acid levels are highest in spring when the snow melts. This is also the time when the young fish hatch from their eggs. They are unable to tolerate the high levels of acidity and die. It is not only the acid in the water that kills them, but also poisonous minerals like aluminium that are leached out of the surrounding ground into the water.

The birds that eat these fish also suffer as the harmful minerals become even more concentrated inside their bodies. The shells of their eggs are more fragile and are liable to break, and when the young birds are hatched, their bones may be deformed.

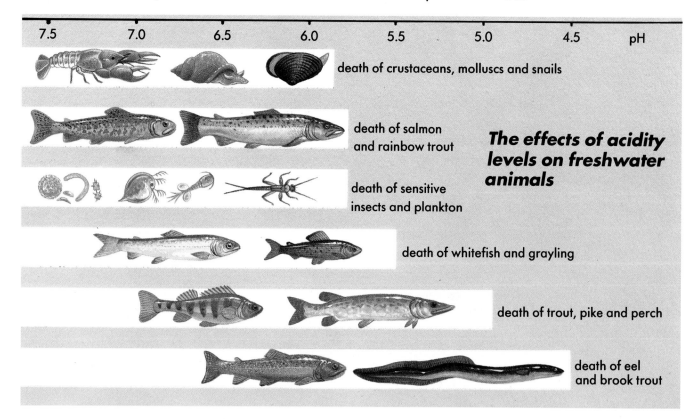

| 7.5 | 7.0 | 6.5 | 6.0 | 5.5 | 5.0 | 4.5 | pH |

death of crustaceans, molluscs and snails

death of salmon and rainbow trout

The effects of acidity levels on freshwater animals

death of sensitive insects and plankton

death of whitefish and grayling

death of trout, pike and perch

death of eel and brook trout

Acid rain and the seas

The seas were once thought not to be affected by acid rain, but a new report from the Environmental Defense Fund (USA) states that acid rain is damaging fish along the Atlantic coast of the USA. Bays and coastal waters which are important fish breeding areas are the worst affected. However, the Reagan administration remained resolutely opposed to any attempts to curb emissions because, it said, there was not enough evidence of damage. In the report, Dr Oppenheimer states 'In ignoring the acid rain problem, Congress and the Administration decided to sacrifice thousands of lakes. As it turns out, they were also pulling the plug on our estuaries and coastal waters'.

There are reports that acid rain is affecting the Atlantic Coast of the USA. Many cities border this coastline, for example New York, which has certainly suffered from acid rain damage.

Damage to trees and forests

It was not until the 1960s that acid rain was recognized as a serious threat to forests. The first evidence was found in the Sudetes, a range of mountains important for timber between Poland and Czechoslovakia. Some of the fir trees had very thin branches and others were dying. By the mid 1970s the problems had become much worse and whole stands of trees were dying, while new ones would not grow.

Timber is an important export for Sweden. However, this industry is threatened by acid rain, which has badly damaged many Swedish forests.

Today, almost 40 per cent of the forest is dead or dying. Large areas that were once covered in forest are now moorland. It did not go unnoticed that the Sudetes lie downwind of an industrial area which relies heavily on brown coal. This releases a lot of sulphur when burnt. The use of brown coal had increased from 30 million tonnes in 1950 to 100 million tonnes in 1980.

This tree in the German Black Forest is suffering from the effects of acid rain. It is producing many cones, indicating that the tree is close to death and is, therefore, trying to generate new trees.

Seed growth and acid rain

You will need:
Seeds (eg clover, peas, mustard, cress), paper cups, potting soil, vinegar, measuring cup, indicator papers, chalk dust.

Plant each type of seed in its own cup filled 2 cm from the top with the soil. Use about 12 cups for each type of seed. Water one third of each group with tap or distilled water and measure its pH. Water the next third with water and vinegar with a pH level of 4.0, and the last third with water and chalk dust to make pH about 8.0. Compare the growth of the seedlings over a period of several weeks. Which seeds grew the best?

Not all areas are so badly affected, but there are reports now from all over the world that trees are suffering. A dead tree is easy to recognize, but in most cases death is not due directly to acid rain. Acid rain weakens trees and they may die when they are blown over or attacked by insects or fungi. Coniferous trees are most at risk, although deciduous trees are also affected.

A German scientist displays a branch of a conifer that has lost many of its needles as a result of acid rain.

How acid rain affects trees

Trees show clear signs of being affected by acid rain. The main symptoms are:

Less foliage: Coniferous trees do not drop their needles annually like deciduous trees. Foresters are able to recognize needles on a healthy tree that are up to 7 years old. Damaged trees lose them more quickly and look very scraggy. Deciduous trees grow less foliage in the summer. One sign of this is that it is possible to see the sky through the tree. These trees also drop their leaves earlier than normal in autumn.

Yellow spots: The sulphur dioxide in the atmosphere causes the needles of conifers to develop yellow spots.

Many cones produced: A damaged conifer close to death produces a great many cones which are the seeds from which new trees can grow.

Die-back: Those parts of the conifer most exposed to acid rain, such as the top and the tips of the branches, lose more needles than the rest of the tree.

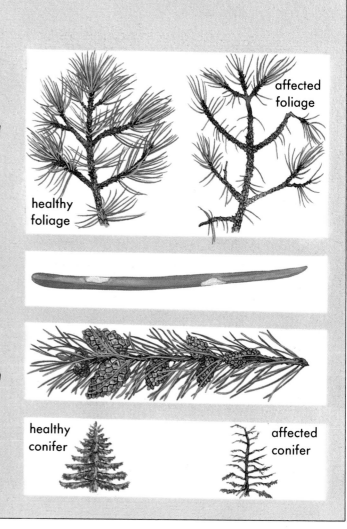

Canadian maple trees are the source of maple syrup but now they are being damaged by acid rain.

Forest damage

'My family has lived on this farm for over 100 years. It covers about 29 hectares, 23 of which are forest. Every year a contractor comes in to fell some of the trees. The older ones are over 100 years old and fetch a high price, as they can be used for timber. However, many of these old trees are now damaged by the acid rain and are dying from insect attacks. A couple of years ago a strong wind blew some of them down. The younger trees will never reach this age. The damage from the acid rain becomes so severe when they are over 50 years old, that I have to fell them while they can still be used as timber instead of wood pulp.'

Ingemar Zachrisson; Sweden

Ingemar Zachrisson explains about acid rain to visitors.

The damage to buildings

If you look at many buildings, especially old ones, you may well notice that the building materials are breaking up. Building materials weather naturally, but over a long period of time, usually many centuries. Acid rain speeds up the process. In 1984, the Statue of Liberty in New York, USA, had to be partially dismantled for restoration because acid pollution had corroded the metal frame and copper covering. Millions of dollars had to be spent to return it to its former glory, but who should pay? Should it be the tax payers of New York or the factories that caused the pollution in the first place?

Below *America's most famous landmark, the Statue of Liberty, being restored in 1984.*

Above *The corrosion of this English church statue has been accelerated by acid rain.*

Can acid rain damage your health?

In some areas, breathing 'fresh' air carries a health warning, especially for the elderly and those who suffer from asthma or other breathing problems, or have a heart problem. In West Germany, the concentrations of sulphur dioxide in the atmosphere have become so dangerous on occasions that people are advised not to go out. In Los Angeles, USA, in 1978, there were 23 days on which some industries had to stop burning coal and oil, while outdoor activities at

In West Germany's industrial area, the Ruhr, smogs can be so serious that traffic diversions are necessary.

school had to be cancelled.

However, following legislation to clean up car exhausts (the major source of this particular pollution) the situation has improved. 1984 was the first year since 1955 that no emergency measures had to be taken. Pollution is therefore not an inevitable result of industrial progress. If we control it, we can all enjoy a healthier life.

Solving the problems

If, having read this far, you are feeling very concerned about the damage being caused to the environment by acid rain, take some heart from the fact that millions of other people feel like you, in Britain, Canada, Norway, Sweden, West Germany, USA, and many other countries. They include young and old, factory workers, farmers, industrialists, politicians, writers, scientists....... in fact, people from all walks of life. It is only a matter of time before everyone will realize the true extent of this problem.

Two of the countries among the most reluctant to accept that acid rain could cause problems, West Germany and Britain, are both taking steps to reduce pollution. West Germany changed its policy almost overnight when it was found that its own forests were suffering badly. West Germany is now one of the leading countries

Reducing sulphur dioxide levels

Signatories to the Geneva Convention	Reduction from 1980 level		
Austria	70%	by	1995
Canada	50%	by	1994
East Germany	30%	by	1993
France	50%	by	1990
Italy	30%	by	1993
Netherlands	50%	by	1995
Norway	50%	by	1994
Sweden	65%	by	1995
United Kingdom	30%	by	1999
USSR	30%	by	1993
West Germany	65%	by	1993

Above *The table lists some of the countries that signed the ECE protocol on air pollution in 1985. By doing so, each country agreed to reduce its emissions of sulphur dioxide by at least 30%.*

Left *A layer of pollution is trapped over the Hüttental valley in West Germany. When the Germans realized that pollution was harming their much-loved forests, they quickly resolved to take preventive action.*

A Swedish lake is limed by helicopter.

pressing for stricter pollution controls. Britain, which is not facing problems as serious as West Germany, would prefer to wait for more conclusive proof. However, it is under pressure from other European governments to take action. The USA is one of the few remaining countries calling for yet more research and debate before it commits itself to taking further action.

It will take a long time before all the causes of acid rain are removed. In the meantime, something has to be done to reduce the impact of acid rain on the environment today.

Liming

You have already read that alkalis help neutralize acids. Lime (crushed limestone) is an alkali and is able to reduce the acidity when put in lakes,

streams or on the land. Lime is most frequently used to reduce the acidity of lakes. The amount needed to restore the acidity to a healthy pH 6.5 varies depending upon the size and acidity of the lake. Typically about 4 tonnes per hectare will be needed to raise the pH from 5.5 to 6.5. After liming, species of plants and animals are quick to return to the lake. As the toxic metals are carried to the bottom of the lake, fish can breed more successfully. The only species to suffer are those that live at the bottom of the lake where the metals accumulate. To prevent the problems from recurring, liming has to be repeated every two to five years. Maintaining lakes in a healthy condition is therefore time-consuming and very expensive, especially in remote areas.

Different ways of applying the lime are tested. In some areas, lime is released constantly into running water, but this requires the use of expensive machinery. In remote areas it is dropped into the water by aeroplane or helicopter. A particularly effective way is spreading the lime over ice-covered lakes in winter. The lime falls into the water when the ice melts in spring – the same time as the acidity increases when all the melt water runs into the lakes. In some areas, lime is spread on the land itself. This is very effective in reducing the acidity of the soil, as well as the water, and is therefore of benefit to the vegetation as well.

The extent of the damage caused by acid rain is so great that liming will never solve the problem. It has been estimated that it would take over 300,000 tonnes of lime a year at a cost of 250 million Norwegian Kroner (about 25 million pounds sterling) to neutralize the acids in southern Norway alone. But locally, the successes are very important.

There are no technical problems in preventing air pollution. The obstacles that have to be overcome are finding the money and, perhaps more importantly, the desire to put a stop to acid rain. Two courses of action are needed. One is to take the practical action needed to reduce emissions of sulphur dioxide and nitrogen oxides. The other is to reach international agreements to make sure that action is taken.

Listed below are some practical ways of reducing the problem of acid rain. You can play your part in solving this problem.

Conservation of energy

The Western way of life involves using a great deal of energy, for example in transport, manufacturing products, heating, lighting and cooking. Yet it has been estimated that if we used the fuel more efficiently and took measures to conserve energy, then we could still enjoy a high standard of living while consuming 50 per cent less energy. The less energy is used, the less pollution is produced.

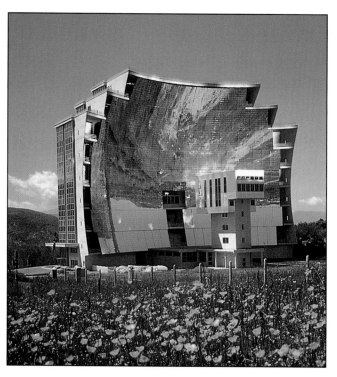

Using alternative sources of energy

Coal, oil and natural gas are used to produce over 75 per cent of the world's energy requirements. These sources will eventually run out. It is possible to use natural sources of energy to generate power which will not run out. These are called renewable sources of energy. They include hydro-electric power (using the power of falling water to drive generators), biomass (burning plant and animal matter), geothermal energy (using natural heat deep in the earth's crust), wave and tidal power from the sea, and wind

Left The solar energy station at Odeillo, France, harnesses the energy of the sun.

Below Windmills are used to generate electricity at this wind farm in California, USA.

This Swiss hydro-electric power station uses water to generate electricity.

power (from windmills). Nuclear power, which creates energy by splitting atoms, is also renewable and does not produce pollutants like sulphur dioxide and nitrogen oxides. However, many people fear the dangers of nuclear accidents and are concerned about the disposal of nuclear waste.

Hydro-electric power is one of the best developed of the renewable resources, providing 25 per cent of the world's electricity. However, this could be increased dramatically with minimum damage to the environment. At present, wind and wave power receive very little money for research and development. However, the wind farms of California, USA, have shown that non-polluting energy can be produced economically and in quantity.

Britain's Drax power station will use a liming process to remove 90% of its sulphur dioxide pollution.

Use of low-sulphur fuels

Not all coal and fuel oils contain a lot of sulphur. By switching to these sources, the amount of pollution could be reduced. But what would be the effect on those areas where people mine fuel with a high sulphur content? Would there be a lot of unemployment?

Removing pollution at source

Sulphur can be removed from fuel before it is burnt, and sold as a by-product to industry. This would actually improve employment prospects in the mining areas, but only if the coal could still be sold at a high price. Alternatively, the sulphur can be removed from the fumes before they are sent into the atmosphere. This can be done using devices called scrubbers positioned in the chimneys. These spray a slurry of limestone through the fumes.

Changing methods of farming and forestry

Farming and forestry can increase the acidity of the soil. If foresters take and use the whole of a tree, including the branches and roots, it is the equivalent of the soil being exposed to acid rain for about 60 years. If only the trunk of a tree is taken, and the rest is left to rot back into the ground, less acidity builds up in the soil.

More and more foresters are leaving the roots and branches of felled trees to rot into the soil. This releases nutrients back into the soil, so improving its ability to suport future forestry plantations.

Changing our behaviour

There are actions that each one of us can take now to reduce pollution problems. By turning down the central heating thermostat by only a couple of degrees, considerably less fuel is used. We could put on extra clothing when cold, instead of turning up the heating. Driving more slowly reduces the amount of nitrogen oxides produced by car engines. In some countries speed limits could be reduced. A limit of about 80 kph seems to be a good compromise between speed and pollution. A great deal of energy and pollution would be saved if more people regularly used public transport systems instead of travelling in their own car.

Traffic jams, such as this one in São Paolo, Brazil, could often be avoided if more people used public transport systems.

Cleaning up vehicle exhausts

Vehicle engines produce nitrogen oxides and other pollutants. Car engine exhausts can be cleaned up by using lead-free petrol and fitting a catalytic converter. These convert 90 per cent of the harmful gases in car exhausts into less harmful carbon dioxide, nitrogen and water vapour. An alternative would be to develop lean-burn engines, which are more efficient and produce less pollution. Diesel engines are cheaper to run because they consume less fuel than petrol engines. However, they produce more smoke – twice as much nitrogen oxide and six times as much sulphur dioxide.

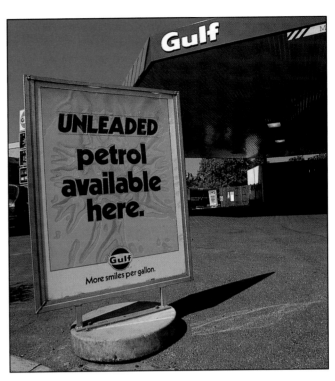

Lead-free petrol is the first step towards cleaner car exhausts.

Car exhaust fumes contain carbon monoxide, nitrogen oxides, sulphur dioxide, and hydrocarbons (unburnt fuel). A catalytic converter would convert most of these substances into carbon dioxide, nitrogen and water vapour.

Some countries, such as the USA and Japan, already have strict laws that control pollution from cars. In the 1990s, EEC regulations will require all cars with engines over two litres to be fitted with catalytic converters. This would dramatically improve the quality of the air. A simple way of avoiding polluting the air is to switch off the car engine when it is not moving. In Switzerland and West Germany, notices at traffic lights instruct drivers to turn off their engines while waiting, rather than allowing them to pour toxic fumes into the air.

Education

Scientists can identify problems and find solutions to them, but unless people in general are aware of the seriousness of the problems, there is little incentive for anyone to take action. Education plays an important part in making people aware of environmental problems.

It costs a lot of money to clean up acid rain. Many countries were reluctant to take action until scientists showed them by how much pollution needs to be cut. Scientists have been doing these calculations for sulphur dioxide and nitrogen oxides and have shown that the more sensitive areas of Norway and Sweden are only capable of absorbing between 0.3-0.5 grammes of sulphur dioxide and 1-2 grammes of nitrogen oxides over a square metre. Levels in many areas of Scandinavia are much higher than this, for example 2-3 grammes of sulphur and 2-3 grammes of nitrogen over a square metre. Scientists estimate that the world as a whole needs to cut down the emissions of these two pollutants by between 80 and 90 per cent. This means that every 100 tonnes currently put into the atmosphere must be reduced to 10 tonnes as soon as possible.

Over the last ten years in Europe, emissions of sulphur dioxide have decreased by about 25 per cent. The total amount falling on Scandinavia has dropped by a similar amount and the good news is that some of the lakes are recovering slightly. Many countries are committed to reducing pollution still further and it is estimated that a further drop of 30 per cent will be achieved by the mid 1990s.

These results have only been achieved because research has been able to show that pollution damages the environment and that pollution is carried by the wind from one country to another. The research will continue, but at the same time countries are working together to try to reduce emissions still further by making agreements with one another.

Members of Greenpeace climbed a German factory chimney to draw attention to the pollution it produces.

Opposite *Members of the European parliament frequently meet together to discuss environmental issues.*

Saving a Swedish lake

'Our lake has been saved by schoolchildren from the city. They came out here on a field course with their teacher and learnt that at one time the lake teemed with wildlife. Then it became acidified, and many species were disappearing. The children wanted to help us save it, so they came back in the winter and helped us spread nine tonnes of lime on the surface of the ice. That summer, when they came back again, they measured the acidity and found that it had fallen from pH 5.7 to pH 6.8. They worked very hard, but they seemed to enjoy themselves as well and are very proud of what they have achieved. We could not have done it so quickly without them.'

Björn Hansen

Reducing nitrogen oxides

Sulphur dioxide is only one of the pollutants causing acid rain problems, but it is the one that has been studied the most. Nitrogen oxides are more complex to study, but in 1986 negotiations started on an international agreement to reduce pollution from nitrogen oxides. There have been problems in reaching agreement on how ambitious the targets should be. West Germany has proposed that there should be a 30 per cent reduction on 1985 nitrogen oxide levels by 1995. This is supported by a number of countries. Britain and France, however, seem to be willing

Los Angeles was one of the first cities to control vehicle pollution, to solve its smog problems.

to go only as far as a 'freeze', which means no further increase in emissions. Italy, Canada, the USA and most eastern European countries appear to be rejecting both proposals.

About 50 per cent of the nitrogen oxides are present in the air as a result of emissions from vehicles. If the amount of pollutants coming from exhausts is reduced, then the total amount of nitrogen oxides in the air is reduced. Japan and the USA are the furthest advanced with strict laws controlling the level of emissions from car exhausts. Drivers in the USA can be stopped, their exhaust tested and the driver forbidden to continue if the exhaust is not clean enough. Perhaps the positive action taken by the USA and Japan will encourage other countries to introduce stricter controls on exhaust fumes.

International developments on emissions of sulphur dioxide

1872 The term 'acid rain' is used for the first time by Robert Smith, Britain's first pollution inspector.

1881 First traces of acid rain noticed in Norway.

1921 Some lakes in southern Norway are found to have no fish in them. Research shows that there is a direct link between fish deaths and the levels of acidity in the lakes.

1950 Interest and concern about acid rain spreads to countries beyond Scandinavia including the USA, Canada, Britain and the USSR.

1970 The USA Clean Air Act leads to the strongest controls in the world to reduce pollution from vehicle exhausts.

1976 OECD (Organization of Economic Cooperation and Development) produces a report stating that pollution produced in one European country is damaging the environment in others.

A network of rain sampling stations is set up in Canada to find out more about acid rain.

1977 The United Nations Economic Commission for Europe (ECE) sets up a programme to monitor long-range pollution.

1978 The National Atmospheric Detection Programme is set up in the USA to find out more about pollution in the atmosphere.

1979 Over 30 countries sign an ECE convention agreeing to reduce atmospheric pollution. However, the wording is very weak because West Germany and Britain do not want controls. The wording they eventually agree to is to 'endeavour to limit and so far as possible gradually reduce and prevent air pollution using the best available technology that is economically feasible'. In other words, if they do not want to do anything, they could always say it would be too expensive.

1980 The USA and Canada sign a declaration of intent to prevent pollution from damaging each other's countries.

1981 OECD publishes a report showing that it would be cheaper to reduce sulphur emissions than to let environmental damage continue.

1982 Canada offers to reduce sulphur dioxide emissions by 50 per cent if USA will do the same. The USA refuses.

1983 West German scientists draw international attention to the link between forest damage and acid rain.

1985 19 countries sign a protocol within the ECE convention and agree to cut sulphur dioxide emissions by 30 per cent. This group became known as 'The 30 per cent Club'. The USA, Poland and Britain do not sign and there are not enough signatories for it to come into effect.

1987 Sufficient countries sign the 30 per cent protocol for it to come into effect. The USA and Britain still do not sign.

1988 End of European Year of the Environment coincides with the European Economic Community's failure to agree plans to cut further the emissions of sulphur dioxide from power stations.

What can we learn from acid rain?

In this book we have seen much evidence that acid rain can damage the environment. But we have also learnt many other things about the environment and ourselves. These will help you when you come to look at other environmental issues.

We have learnt that not everyone agrees about the causes of environmental damage or the solutions needed. Some say there is still not enough evidence that acid rain damages the environment. Based upon the information you can collect from other sources, you will have to make up your own mind. Before you reach conclusions about any environmental issue, you should consider all the evidence available for each point of view.

You have also learnt that, left to themselves, plants and animals achieve an ecological balance. From one year to the next, the environment of the wood, the lake, the moor or the desert does not change very much. Very many species, including humans, live and depend on one another in these environments. Yet we are the only species that has the ability to change the environment significantly. Sometimes our activities upset the balance so much that the environment is damaged. However, we can also work with nature to protect the environment, while still using it to meet our very many needs.

Sometimes the evidence that pollution harms the environment is hard to deny.

This notice in a Tokyo street displays levels of noise and air pollution.

It is people who finally determine the kind of environment in which you have to live. We all share the responsibility to care for our planet. It is easy to blame others for creating an environment we do not like but have we damaged it by our own actions? Think about this and decide if you would like to do something to protect our environment. You can help by saving energy, as suggested in a previous chapter, or you may like to join an environmental organization. Some useful addresses are listed at the back of this book, and your teacher will also be able to give you some advice.

A cleaner environment means cleaner cities and healthy trees and lakes for all to enjoy.

Glossary

Acid A solution with a pH value of less than 7.0. It is capable of neutralizing an alkali.

Alkali A solution capable of neutralizing an acid. It has a pH value greater than 7.0.

Atmosphere The gaseous layer that surrounds the earth. Not counting water vapour, it consists of nitrogen (78 per cent), oxygen (21 per cent), argon (1 per cent) and very tiny amounts of carbon dioxide, neon, ozone, hydrogen, krypton and pollutants. Water vapour generally represents between 1 and 4 per cent of the atmosphere.

Brown coal Dead vegetation that has not been fully compressed to become coal.

Buffer The ability of soils and water to neutralize or partly neutralize acid precipitation.

Catalytic converter A device fitted to car exhausts to remove pollution.

Convention An agreement made by a group of countries to work together towards a common goal.

Ecosystem A community of plants and animals and the environment in which they live.

Emissions Substances discharged into the air from chimneys and vehicle exhausts.

Environment A plant's or animal's surroundings, including the air, water, soil and rock types.

Fossil fuels Fuels derived from organic substances, for example coal, oil and natural gas.

Heavy metals Metals like cadmium, aluminium and mercury, which are found in the soil and are poisonous to plants and animals.

Leaching The process by which water moves minerals from one layer of soil to another, or into streams.

Liming Dumping alkaline substances, such as crushed limestone, into water courses, lakes or on to the ground. This is done to neutralize high levels of acidity.

Neutralize To reduce the level of acidity in a substance, so that it becomes neither acid nor alkaline (pH 7).

Nitrogen oxides (NOx) Gases formed mainly from nitrogen in the atmosphere when fuels are burnt at a high temperature.

Organic material Matter that is living or was once living.

Organism Any animal or plant which can sustain life by itself.

Ozone A form of oxygen that can damage plant growth and irritate the eyes and breathing system. However, ozone forms a vital layer of the atmosphere, shielding the earth from the sun's harmful ultra-violet rays.

pH The unit for measuring acidity.

Pollutants Substances which can damage the air, water or the land when released into it.

Pollution The presence of harmful substances in the environment.

Prevailing wind The direction from which the wind most often blows.

Protocol An agreement that is part of a convention.

Precipitation Moisture that falls to the earth such as rain, sleet, snow or mist.

Scrubber A device attached to a chimney that sprays a liquid through the gases to remove pollutants like sulphur dioxide.

Sulphur dioxide (SO2) A strong-smelling, colourless gas formed mainly from the burning of fossil fuels.

Toxic Harmful or poisonous.

United Nations The international organization that brings all the countries of the world together to discuss, and attempt to solve, world problems.

Further reading

Acid Magazine National Swedish Environment Protection Board.
A popular science magazine which provides up-to date information on acidification and air pollution. Issued twice a year.

Acid Rain National Society for Clean Air
A 6-page leaflet explaining acid rain, its effects on the environment, what can be done to control it and the legislative measures taken to reduce harmful emissions.

Acid Rain Schools Information Centre on the Chemical Industry, Polytechnic of North London, Holloway Road, London N7 8DB
An information booklet for schools.

Acid Rain World Wide Fund for Nature.
A newspaper-style information sheet presenting the facts about acidification and what is being done to prevent it.

Acidification and Air Pollution National Swedish Environmental Protection Board 1987.
A small book giving a comprehensive coverage of the acid problem.

Acid Deposition American Society for Environmental Education (1986).
An issue of their journal for education about acid rain.

Air Ecology, Jennifer Cochrane (Wayland 1987)

The Environment, World Issues series, Adam Markham (Wayland, 1988)

Pollution and the Environment, Mary Lean (Macdonald, 1985)

Stop Acid Rain The Stop Acid Rain Campaign, Norway 1986.
A booklet describing the history and effects of acid rain and solving acid rain problems.

Water Ecology, Jennifer Cochrane (Wayland 1987)
An informative, acitivity-based book looking at how living things affect and are affected by, their environment.

Useful addresses

The Acid Rain Foundation
1630 Blackhawk Hills
St Paul MN 55122
USA

Aims to develop and raise public awareness of the issue and supplies educational resources.

Acid Rain Information Centre
Department of Environmental and Geographic Studies
Manchester Polytechnic
Chester Street
Manchester M1 5GD
Britain

Collects information from concerned organizations in Britain and abroad. Postal enquiries answered if stamped, self-addressed envelope included. There is also a speaker service, videos for hire and a display available.

Acid Rain Information Clearing House
Centre for Environmental Information Inc.
33 S. Washington Street
Rochester
NY 14608
USA

Provides general information about acid rain.

British Coal
Public Relations Department
Hobart House
Grosvenor Place
London SW1X 7AE
Britain

Provides information for education.

Central Electricity Generating Board
Sudbury House
15 Newgate Street
London EC1A 7AU
Britain

Operates power stations and conducts research into all environmental problems connected with power generation. Publishes booklets, leaflets and films.

Friends of the Earth
377 City Road
London EC1V 1NA
Britain

An environmental pressure group which campaigns for conservation, environmental improvement and a wise use of resources. Booklets and pamphlets are available.

National Society for Clean Air
136 North Street
Brighton
BN1 1RG
Britain

Promotes public education in all matters relating to the quality of the air.

National Swedish Environment Protection Board
Information Section
Box 1302
S-171 25
Solna
Sweden

Co-ordinates the Swedish campaign against acid rain. Provides information, journals and films.

Sierra Club
730 Polk Street
San Francisco
CA 94109
USA

Publishes a regular newsletter with details of environmental legislation in USA.

The Stop Acid Rain Campaign
IMSN, c/o Det Norske Skogselskap
Werdelandsvn. 23b
0167 Oslo 1
Norway

Provides information on acid rain including books and magazines.

Watch
22 The Green
Nettleham
Lincs LN2 2NR
Britain

A national club which enables young people to increase their knowledge of wildlife and to take an active part in conservation. Organized the Acid Drops and ozone projects.

World Wide Fund for Nature
WWF Information and Education Division
1196 Gland
Switzerland

Produces information for education about acid rain.

Picture acknowledgements

The publishers would like to thank the following for allowing their photographs to be reproduced in this book: John Baines 23 below, 28; Bruce Coleman Limited 4 (Wayne Lankinen), 5 above (John Shaw),inset (Kim Taylor),6 (John Brownlie), 8 above (Steve Kaufman), 11 (George McCarthy), 12 (Colin Molyneux), 15 (P A Hinchliffe), 18 (John Shaw), 21 (Hans Reinhard), 23 above, 24 above (Adrian Davies), below (Norman Tomalin), 25 (N Schwartz), 34 (Norman Owen), 40 (Colin Molyneux);CEGB/DIPA Photo Library 32; Greenpeace 36; ICCE 22 (Rod Redknapp) 35 above (Mark Boulton); Andre Maslennikov/IBL Sweden 16, 27; Oxford Scientific Films 14 (G A MaClean), 29 (Steve Littlewood); Rex Features 37 (Boccon); Science Photo Library 30 above (Gazuit); Topham Picture Library 41; ZEFA 8 below, 10 (Hunter), 17 (Adam), 19, 20 (Mosler), 26 (M Becker), 30 below (T Braise), 31 (Bramaz), 33 (Hunter), 35 below (H Schmid), 38 (G Juckes), 42. The illustrations are by Jane Pickering 18, 22; Malcolm Walker 7; and Brian Watson 6, 9, 13, 15, 21.

Index